MOLLY SWEENEY

BY BRIAN FRIEL

★

★

DRAMATISTS
PLAY SERVICE
INC.

MOLLY SWEENEY
Copyright © 1994, 1995, 1996, Brian Friel

All Rights Reserved

SPECIAL NOTE

MOLLY SWEENEY was first produced at The Gate Theatre, Dublin
Michael Colgan, Artistic Director
Subsequently produced by The Gate Theatre at the Almeida Theatre, London
New York Premiere at the Laura Pels Theatre, presented by The Roundabout
Theatre Company, The Gate Theatre, Dublin, Ireland,
and Emanuel Azenberg.

For Megan

ACKNOWLEDGMENT

I am particularly indebted to Oliver Sacks'
case history "To See and Not See,"
and the long, strange tradition
of such case histories

MOLLY SWEENEY had its New York premiere on December 26, 1995, at the Laura Pels Theatre, presented by The Roundabout Theatre Company (Todd Haimes, Artistic Director), The Gate Theatre, Dublin, Ireland (Michael Colgan, Artistic Director), and Emanuel Azenberg. It was directed by Brian Friel; the set and costume designs were by Joe Vanek; the lighting design was by Mick Hughes and the production managers were Philip Cusack and John Vivian. The cast was as follows:

MOLLY SWEENEY.. Catherine Byrne
MR. RICE..Jason Robards
FRANK SWEENEY .... Alfred Molina

MOLLY SWEENEY was first produced at the Gate Theatre (Michael Colgan, Artistic Director) in Dublin, Ireland, on August 9, 1994 and subsequently produced by The Gate Theatre at the Almeida Theatre, London, England, on November 3, 1994. It was directed by Brian Friel; the set design was by Joe Vanek; the costume design was by Joan Bergin and the lighting design was by Mick Hughes. The cast was as follows:

MOLLY SWEENEY.. Catherine Byrne
MR. RICE.. T. P. McKenna
FRANK SWEENEY ....Mark Lambert

Tell all the Truth but tell it slant —
Success in Circuit lies
Too bright for our infirm Delight
The Truth's superb surprise
As Lightning to the Children eased
With explanation kind
The Truth must dazzle gradually
Or every man be blind

Emily Dickinson

"Learning to see is not like learning a new language. It's like learning language for the first time."

Denis Diderot

MOLLY SWEENEY

ACT ONE

When the lights go up, we discover three characters —
MOLLY SWEENEY, MR. RICE, FRANK SWEENEY — on
stage. All three stay on stage for the entire play.

I suggest that each character inhabits his/her own special act-
ing area — MR. RICE stage left, MOLLY SWEENEY cen-
tre stage, FRANK SWEENEY stage right (left and right from
the point of view of the audience).

MOLLY SWEENEY and FRANK SWEENEY are in their late
thirties — early forties. MR. RICE is older. Most people with
impaired vision look and behave like fully sighted people. The
only evidence of their disability is usually a certain vacancy
in their eyes, or the way the head is held. MOLLY should
indicate her disability in some such subtle way. No canes,
no groping, no dark glasses, etc.

MOLLY.   By the time I was five years of age, my father had
taught me the names of dozens of flowers and herbs and
shrubs and trees. He was a judge and his work took him all
over the county. And every evening, when he got home, after
he'd had a few quick drinks, he'd pick me up in his arms and
carry me out to the walled garden.

"Tell me now," he'd ask, "Where precisely are we?"

"We're in your garden."

"Oh, you're such a clever little missy!" And he'd pretend to smack me.

"Exactly what part of my garden?"

"We're beside the stream."

"Stream? Do you hear a stream? I don't. Try again."

"We're under the lime tree."

"I smell no lime tree. Sorry. Try again."

"We're beside the sundial."

"You're guessing. But you're right. And at the bottom of the pedestal there is a circle of petunias. There are about twenty of them all huddled together in one bed. They are — what? — seven inches tall. Some of them are blue-and-white, and some of them are pink, and a few have big, red, cheeky faces. Touch them."

And he would bend over, holding me almost upside down, and I would have to count them and smell them and feel their velvet leaves and their sticky stems. Then he'd test me.

"Now, Molly. Tell me what you saw."

"Petunias."

"How many petunias did you see?"

"Twenty."

"Colour?"

"Blue-and-white and pink and red."

"Good. And what shape is their bed?"

"It's a circle."

"Splendid. Passed with flying colours. You *are* a clever lady."

And to have got it right for him and to hear the delight in his voice gave me such pleasure.

Then we'd move on to his herb bed and to his rose bed and to his ageratum and his irises and his azaleas and his sedum. And when we'd come to his nemophila, he always said the same thing.

"Nemophila are sometimes called Baby Blue Eyes. I know you can't see them but they have beautiful blue eyes. Just like you. You're my nemophila."

And then we'd move onto the shrubs and the trees and we'd perform the same ritual of naming and counting and touching and smelling. Then, when our tour was ended,

10

he'd kiss my right cheek and then my left cheek with that old-world formality with which he did everything; and I loved that because his whiskey breath made my head giddy for a second.

"Excellent!" he'd say. "Excellent testimony! We'll adjourn until tomorrow."

Then if mother were away in hospital with her nerves, he and I would make our own meal. But if she were at home she'd appear at the front door — always in her headscarf and Wellingtons — and she'd shout, "Molly! Daddy! Dinner!" I never heard her call him anything but Daddy and the word always seemed to have a mocking edge. And he'd say to me, "Even scholars must eat. Let us join your mother."

And sometimes, just before we'd go into that huge, echoing house, sometimes he'd hug me to him and press his mouth against my ear and whisper with fierce urgency, "I promise you, my darling, you aren't missing a lot; not a lot at all. Trust me."

Of course I trusted him; completely. But late at night, listening to mother and himself fighting their weary war downstairs and then hearing him grope his way unsteadily into bed, I'd wonder what he meant. And it was only when I was about the same age as he was then, it was only then that I thought — I thought perhaps I was beginning to understand what he meant. But that was many, many years later. And by then mother and he were long dead and the old echoing house was gone. And I had been married to Frank for over two years. And by then, too, I had had the operation on the first eye.

MR. RICE. The day he brought her to my house — the first time I saw them together — my immediate thought was: what an unlikely couple!

I had met him once before about a week earlier; by himself. He had called to ask would I see her, just to give an opinion, if only to confirm that nothing could be done for her. I suggested he phone the hospital and make an appointment in the usual way. But of course he didn't. And within two hours he was back at my door again with an enormous folder of material that had to do with her case and that he had compiled over the years and he'd be happy to go through it with me there and then because not only were the documents and reports and photographs interesting in themselves but they would be essential reading for someone like myself who was going to take her case on.

Yes, an ebullient fellow; full of energy and enquiry and the indiscriminate enthusiasms of the self-taught. And convinced, as they usually are, that his own life story was of compelling interest. He had worked for some charitable organisation in Nigeria. Kept goats on an island off the Mayo coast and made cheese. Sold storage batteries for those windmill things that produce electricity. Endured three winters in Norway to ensure the well-being of whales. That sort of thing. Worthy pursuits, no doubt. And he was an agreeable fellow; oh, yes; perfectly agreeable. Frank. That was his name. She was Molly. Reminded me instantly of my wife, Maria. Perhaps the way she held her head. A superficial resemblance. Anyhow. Molly and Frank Sweeney.

I liked her. I liked her calm and her independence; the confident way she shook my hand and found a seat for herself with her white cane. And when she spoke of her disability, there was no self-pity, no hint of resignation. Yes, I liked her.

Her life, she insisted, was uneventful compared with his. An only child. Father a judge. Mother in and out of institutions all her days with nervous trouble. Brought up by various housekeepers. For some reason she had never been sent to a blind school. Said she didn't know why; perhaps because her father thought he could handle the situation best at home.

She had been blind since she was ten months old. She wasn't totally sightless; she could distinguish between light and dark; she could see the direction from which light came; she could detect the shadow of Frank's hand moving in front of her face. But for all practical purposes she had no useful sight. Other ophthalmologists she had been to over the years had all agreed that surgery would not help. She had a full life and never felt at all deprived. She was now forty-one, married just over two years and working as a massage therapist in a local health club. Frank and she had met there and had married within a month. They were fortunate they had her earnings to live on because he was out of work at the moment.

She offered this information matter-of-factly. And as she talked, he kept interrupting. "She knows when I pass my hand in front of her face. So there is some vision, isn't there? So there is hope, isn't there, isn't there?" Perhaps, I said. "And if there is a chance, any chance, that she might be able to see, we must take it, mustn't we? How can we not take it? She has nothing to lose, has she? What has she to lose? — nothing! — nothing!"

And she would wait without a trace of impatience until he had finished and then she would go on. Yes, I liked her at once.

His 'essential' folder. Across it he had written, typically, RESEARCHED AND COMPILED BY FRANK C. SWEENEY. The 'C' stood for Constantine, I discovered. And it did have some interest, the folder. Photographs of her cycling by herself across a deserted beach. Results of tests she had undergone years ago. A certificate for coming first in her physiotherapy exams. Pictures of them on their honeymoon in Stratford-on-Avon — his idea of self-improvement, no doubt. Letters from two specialists she had been to in her late teens. An article he had cut out of a magazine about miraculous ophthalmological techniques once practised in Tibet — or was it Mongolia? Diplomas she had won in provincial swimming championships. And remarkably — in his own furious handwriting — remarkably extracts from essays by various philosophers on the relationship between vision and knowledge, between seeing and understanding. A strange fellow, indeed.

And when I talked to them on that first occasion I saw them together in my house, I knew that she was there at Frank's insistence, to please him, and not with any expectation that I could help. And as I watched her sitting there, erect in her seat and staring straight ahead, two thoughts flitted across my mind. That her blindness was his latest cause and that it would absorb him just as long as his passion lasted. And then, I wondered, what then? But perhaps that was too stern a judgment.

And the second and much less worthy thought I had was this. No, not a thought; a phantom desire, a fantasy in my head; absurd, bizarre, because I knew only the barest outlines of her case, hadn't even examined her yet; the thought, the bizarre thought that perhaps, perhaps — up here in Donegal — not in Paris or Dallas or Vienna or Milan — but perhaps up here in remote Ballybeg was I about to be given — what is the vulgar parlance? — the chance of a lifetime, the one-in-a-thousand opportunity that can rescue a career — no, no, transform a career — dare I say it, restore a reputation? And if that opportunity were being offered to me and if after all these years I could pull myself together and measure up to it, and if, Oh my God if by some miracle pull it off perhaps ... *(He laughs in self-mockery.)*

Yes, I'm afraid so. People who live alone frequently enjoy an opulent fantasy life.

FRANK.   One of the most fascinating discoveries I made when I was in the cheese business — well, perhaps not fascinating, but interesting, definitely interesting — one of the more interesting discoveries I made — this was long before I met Molly — for three and a half years I had a small goat farm on the island of Inis Beag off the Mayo coast — no, no not a farm for small goats — a farm for ordinary goats — well, extraordinary goats as a matter of fact because I imported two piebald Iranian goats; and the reason I wanted them, the reason I wanted Iranians, was that in all the research I had done and according to all the experts they were reputed to give the highest milk yield — untrue as it turned out — and because their pelts were in great demand as wall coverings in California — equally untrue, I'm afraid; and although they bred very successfully — eventually I had a herd of fourteen — they couldn't endure the Mayo winters with the result that I had to keep them indoors and feed them for six months of the year — in Mayo the winter lasts for six months for God's sake — and of course that threw my whole financial planning into disarray. As you can imagine. And yes, as a matter of interest, they are small animals, Iranian goats. And, as I say, from Iran which, as you know, is an ancient civilization on South West ... Asia ...

But I was telling you about — what? The interesting discovery? Yes! Well, perhaps not an interesting discovery in any general sense but certainly of great interest to anybody who hopes to make cheese from the milk of imported Iranian goats, not that there are thousands of those people up and down the country! Anyhow — anyhow — what I discovered was this. I had those goats for three and a half years, and even after all that time their metabolism, their internal clock, stayed Iranian; never adjusted to Irish time. Their system never made the transition. They lived in a kind of perpetual jet-lag.

So what, you may ask? So for three and a half years I had to get up to feed them at three in the morning my time because that was 7:00 A.M. their time, their breakfast time! And worse — worse — they couldn't be kept awake and consequently couldn't be milked after eight in the evening because that was midnight their time — and they were lying there, dead out, snoring! Bizarre! Some imprint in the genes remained indelible and immutable. I read a brilliant article once by a professor in an American magazine and he called this imprint an engram, from the Greek word meaning something that is etched, inscribed, on something. He said it accounts for the mind's strange ability to recognise instantly somebody we haven't seen for maybe thirty years. Then he appears. The sight of him connects with the imprint, the engram. And bingo — instant recognition!

Interesting word — engram. The only other time I heard it used was by Mr. Rice, Molly's ophthalmologist. In that swanky Yankee accent of his — 'engram'. And he was born in the village of Kilmeedy in County Limerick for God's sake! I really never did warm to that man. No wonder his wife cleared off with another man. No, no, no, I don't mean that; I really don't mean that; that's a rotten thing to say; sorry; I shouldn't have said that. But I was talking about the word engram and how he pronounced it. That was before any of the operations, and he was explaining that to Molly that if by some wonderful, miraculous good fortune her sight were restored, even partially restored, she would still have to learn to see and that would be an enormous and very difficult undertaking.

The way he explained it was this. She knew dozens of flowers; not to see; not by sight. She knew them only if she could touch them and smell them because those tactile engrams were implanted in her brain since she was a child. But if she weren't allowed to touch, to smell, she wouldn't know one flower from another; she wouldn't know a flower from a football. How could she?

And interestingly, interestingly, this very same problem was debated three hundred years ago by two philosophers, William Molyneux and his friend, John Locke. I came across this discussion in a Do-It-Yourself magazine of all places! Fascinating stuff, philosophy — absolutely fascinating. Anyhow — anyhow. If you are blind, said Molyneux, if you are blind you can learn to distinguish between a cube and a sphere just by touching them, by feeling them. Right! Right. Now, supposing your vision is suddenly restored, will you be able — by sight alone, without touching, without feeling — will you be able to tell which object is the cube and which the sphere? Sorry, friend, says Locke, you will not be able to tell which is which.

Then who comes along to join in the debate but another philosopher, Bishop George Berkeley, with his essay titled "An Essay Towards a New Theory of Vision." When the problem was put to the Lord Bishop, he came to the same conclusion as his friends. But he went even further. He said that there was no necessary connection *at all* between the tactile world — the world of touch — and the world of sight; and that any connection between the two could be established only by living, only by experience, only by learning the connection.

Which indeed, is really what Rice said to Molly three hundred years later. That most of us are born with all five senses; and with all the information they give us, we build up a sight world from the day we are born — a world of objects and ideas and meanings. We aren't given that world, he said. We make it ourselves — through our experience, by our memory, by making categories, by interconnections. Now Molly had only ten months of sight and what she had seen in that time was probably forgotten. So, if her sight were restored, everything would have to be learned anew: she would have to *learn* to see. She would have to build up a whole repertory of visual engrams and then, then she would have to establish connections between these new imprints and the tactile engrams she already possessed. Put it another way: she would have to create a whole new world of her own.

How in God's name did I get into all that? The goats! Engrams! Three o'clock every bloody morning! I'll tell you something: three and a half years on that damned island and I lost three stone weight. And not an ounce of cheese — ever!

Not that it mattered, I suppose. I didn't go into Inis Beag to make my fortune. God knows why I went. God knows why I've spent my life at dozens of mad schemes. Crazy ... Billy Hughes — Billy's an old pal of mine — Billy says I'm haunted for God's sake, always looking for ... whatever ...

Anyhow — anyhow. To go back for a second to our friend who knew what a cube was by touching it but couldn't identify it by sight alone. Rice talked a lot to Molly about all that stuff. He said neurologists had a word for people in that condition — seeing but not knowing, not recognising, what it is they see. He said that people in that condition are called agnosic. Yes. Agnosic. Strange; because I always thought that word had to do with believing or not believing.

MOLLY.   I didn't like Mr. Rice when I first met him. But I got to like him. I suppose because I trusted him. Frank never warmed to him. He was put off by his manner and the way he spoke. But I thought that for all his assurance there was something ... unassured about him.

He was said to have been one of the most brilliant ophthalmologists ever in the country. Worked in the top eye hospitals all over the world — Japan, Germany. Spent years in America. Married a Swiss girl. They had two daughters. Then she left him — according to the gossip; went off with a colleague of his from New York. The daughters lived with her parents in Geneva. For years after that there are gaps in his story. Nobody seems to know what became of him. They say that he had a breakdown; that he worked as a labourer in Bolivia; that he ran a pub in Glasgow. Anyhow he turned up here in Ballybeg and got a job in the hospital and took a rented bungalow at the outskirts of the town. He looked after himself in a sort of way. Walked a bit. Did a lot of fly-fishing during the season — Frank said he was beautiful to watch. People thought him a bit prickly, a bit uppity, but that was probably because he didn't mix much. I'm sure a brilliant man like that never thought he'd end up in a regional hospital in the north-west of Donegal. When I wondered what he looked like I imagined a face with an expression of some bewilderment.

Maybe I liked him because of all the doctors who examined me over the years he was the only one who never quizzed me about what it felt like to be blind — I suppose because he knew everything about it. The others kept asking me what the idea of colour meant to me, or the idea of space, or the notion of distance. You live in a world of touch, a tactile world, they'd say. You depend almost entirely on tactile perceptions, on knowing things by feeling their shape. Tell us: how do you think your world compares with the world the rest of us know, the world you would share with us if you had visual perception as well?

He never asked me questions like that. He did ask me once did the idea, the possibility, of seeing excite me or frighten me. It certainly excited Frank, I said. But why should it be frightening? A stupid question, I know, he said. Very stupid.

Why indeed should it be frightening? And how could I answer all those other questions? I knew only my own world.

I didn't think of it as a deprived world. Disadvantaged in some ways; of course it was. But at that stage I never thought of it as deprived. And Mr. Rice knew that.

And how could I have told those other doctors how much pleasure my world offered me? — from my work, from the radio, from walking, from music, from cycling. But especially from swimming. Oh, I can't tell you the joy I got from swimming. I used to think — and I know this sounds silly — but I really did believe I got more pleasure, more delight, from swimming than sighted people can ever get. Just offering yourself to the experience — every pore open and eager for that world of pure sensation, of sensation alone — sensation that could not have been enhanced by sight — experience that existed only by touch and feel; and moving swiftly and rhythmically through that enfolding world; and the sense of such assurance, such liberation, such concordance with it.... Oh, I can't tell you the joy swimming gave me. I used to think that the other people in the pool with me, the sighted people, that in some way their pleasure was actually diminished because they could see, because seeing in some way qualified the sensation; and that if they only knew how full, how total my pleasure was, I used to tell myself that they must, they really must envy me.

Silly, I suppose. Of course it was. I tried to explain how I felt to Mr. Rice.

"I know what you mean," he said.

And I think he did know.

Yes, maybe he was a bit pompous. And he could be sarcastic at times. And Frank said he didn't look at all bewildered; ever. But although I never saw my father's face, I imagine it never revealed any bewilderment either.

MR. RICE.   In the present state of medicine nothing can be done for people who are born blind, the clinically blind. Their retinas are totally insensitive to light and so are non-functional. There are no recorded cases of recovery from clinical blindness.

19

Molly Sweeney wasn't born blind. She was functionally blind and lived in a blind world for forty years. But she wasn't clinically blind: her retinas weren't totally insensitive to light. For God's sake how often did the husband, Mr. Autodidact, tell me that she was aware of the shadow of his hand in front of her face?

So, in theory, perhaps — purely theoretically — her case wasn't exactly hopeless. But I did make a point of giving her and her husband the only statistic available to us; and a dispiriting statistic it is. The number of cases known to us — of people who became blind shortly after birth and had their sight restored many years later — the number of cases over the past ten centuries is not more than twenty. Twenty people in a thousand years.

I know she believed me. I wasn't at all sure Frank Constantine did.

Anyhow, as a result of that first cursory examination in my home, I decided to bring her into the clinic for tests.

FRANK. Well of course the moment Rice said in that uppity voice of his, "In theory — in theory — perhaps in theory" — the first time Molly met him — after a few general questions, a very quick examination — ten o'clock in the morning in his house — I'll never forget it — the front room in the rented bungalow — no fire — the remains of last night's supper on a tray in the fireplace — teapot, crusts, cracked mug — well of course, goddammit, of course the head exploded! Just exploded!

Molly was going to see! I knew it! For all his perhapses! Absolutely no doubt about it! A new world — a new life! A new life for both of us!

MIRACLE OF MOLLY SWEENEY. GIFT OF SIGHT RESTORED TO MIDDLE-AGED WOMAN.

"*I'VE BEEN GIVEN A NEW WORLD,*" SAYS MRS. SWEENEY;

UNEMPLOYED HUSBAND CRIES OPENLY. And why not?

Oh my God ...

Sight ...

I saw an Austrian psychiatrist on the television one night. Brilliant man. Brilliant lecture. He said that when the mind is confronted by a situation of overwhelming intensity — a moment of terror or ecstasy or tragedy — to protect itself from overload, from overcharge, it switches off and focuses on some trivial detail associated with the experience.

And he was right. I know he was. Because that morning in that front room in the chilly bungalow — immediately after that moment of certainty, that explosion in the head — my mind went numb; fused; and all I could think of was that there was a smell of fresh whiskey off Rice's breath. And at ten o'clock in the morning that seemed the most astonishing thing in the world and I could barely stop myself from saying to Molly, "Do you not smell the whiskey off his breath? The man's reeking of whiskey!"

Ridiculous ...

MR. RICE.   Tests revealed that she had thick cataracts on both eyes. But that wasn't the main problem. She also had retinitis pigmentosa; as the name suggests a discolouration of the retina. She seemed to have no useful retinal function. It wasn't at all surprising that other doctors had been put off.

There were scars of old disease, too. But what was encouraging — to put it at its very best — was that there was no current, no active disease process. So that if I were to decide to operate and if the operation were even partially successful, her vision, however impaired, ought to be stable for the rest of her life.

So in theory perhaps ...

FRANK.   On the morning of Tuesday, October the 7th, he operated on the right eye to remove a cataract and implant a new lens.

I was told not to visit her until the following day because the eye would be bandaged for twenty-four hours and she had to have as much rest and quiet as possible. Naturally, of course ...

And a wonderful thing happened that night when I was at home by myself. I got a call from London; from a friend I knew in Nigeria in the old days. Chap called Winterman, Dick Winterman. Inviting me to set up and supervise a food convoy to Ethiopia. Was I interested?

Of course I was interested. The first job I'd been offered in months. But not now. How could I go now for God's sake? Molly was on the verge of a new life. I had to be with her now. Anyhow, as I told Dick, those rambling days were over.

All the same it was nice to be remembered. And to be remembered on that night — I thought that was a good omen.

MR. RICE. I'm ashamed to say that within a week I crossed the frontier into the fantasy life again. The moment I decided I was going to operate on Molly I had an impulse — a dizzying, exuberant, overmastering, intoxicating instinct to phone Roger Bloomstein in New York and Hans Girder in Berlin and Hiroshi Matoba in Kyoto — even old Murnahan in Dublin — and tell them what I was about to do. Yes, yes, especially old Murnahan in Dublin; and say to him, "Paddy Rice here, Professor. Of course you remember him! You called him a rogue star once — oh, yes, that caused a titter. Well, he works in a rundown hospital in Donegal now. And I suspect, I think, I believe for no good reason at all that Paddy Rice is on the trembling verge, Professor. He has a patient who has been blind for forty years. And do you know what? He is going to give her vision — the twenty-first recorded case in over a thousand years! And for the first time in her life — how does Saint Mark put it in the gospel? — for the first time in her life she will 'see men walking as if like trees.'

Delirium ... hubris ... the rogue star's token insurrection ... a final, ridiculous flourish. For God's sake, a routine cataract operation?

Of course I made no calls. Instead I wrote to my daughters, Aisling and Helga, in Geneva, and enclosed what money I could afford. Then to Maria, my ex-wife, in New York; yet another open-heart letter, full of candour and dreary honesty. I told her I was busy and in good spirits and involved in a new case that was unusual in some respects.

Then I made supper; had a few drinks; fell asleep in the armchair. I woke again at 4:00 A.M., my usual hour, and sat there waiting for a new day, and said to myself over and over again: why the agitation over this case? You remove cataracts every day of the week, don't you? And isn't the self-taught husband right? *(Angrily.)* What has she to lose for Christ's sake? Nothing! Nothing at all!

MOLLY.   What a party we had the night before the operation! Three o'clock in the morning before we got the house cleared. Oh, God! And I had to be in the hospital for ten — fasting. Frank wanted to get a taxi but I said we should walk to get all that alcohol out of the system.

And it wasn't that we had organised anything that night. A few neighbours just dropped in to wish me luck; and then a few more; and then Frank said, "Come on! This is beginning to feel like a wake!"; and away he went to the off-licence and came back with a load of stuff.

Who was there? Tony and Betty from this side; with Molly, their baby; they called her after me; she was just a toddler then. And the Quinns from that side; Jack and Mary. Jack wasn't drinking for some reason and Mary certainly was; so that was a delicate situation. And old Mr. O'Neill from across the street; first time outside his house since his wife, Louise, died three months before; and Frank just took him by the arm and said he would fall into a decline if he didn't pull himself together. Anyhow, after two or three beers, what does Mr. O'Neill do? Up on top of the table and begins reciting *"A Bunch of the Boys Were Whooping It Up in the Malamute Saloon"* — or whatever the right name is! Yes! Little timid Mr. O'Neill, the mourning widower! Somebody told me recently that he's in a hospice now.

Who else? Billy Hughes was there; an old bachelor friend of Frank's. Years ago Frank and he borrowed money from the bank and bought forty beehives; but I gather that didn't work out. And Dorothy and Joyce; they're physiotherapists in the hospital. And Tom McLaughlin, another of Frank's bachelor friends. He's a great fiddler, Tom. And that was it. And of course Rita, Rita Cairns, my oldest, my closest friend. She managed the health club I was working in. Rita probably knows me better than anybody.

There was a lot of joking that there were thirteen of us if you counted the baby. And Billy Hughes, who was already well tanked by the time he arrived, he suggested that maybe Jack — from that side — maybe Jack would do the decent and volunteer to leave since he was in a bad mood and wasn't drinking anyway. And Mary, Jack's wife, she said that was the brightest idea all evening. So that was an even trickier situation.

And at some point in the night — it must have been about two — I'm afraid I had a brainwave. Here we are, all friends together, having a great time; so shouldn't I phone Mr. Rice and ask him to join us? Wasn't he a friend, too? And I made for the phone and dialed the number. But Frank, thank God, Frank pulled the phone out of my hand before he answered. Imagine the embarrassment that would have been!

Anyway we chatted and we played tapes and we sang and we drank. And Tony and Betty from this side, Molly's parents, they sang, "Anything You Can Do I Can Do Better" and there was so much tension between them you knew they weren't performing at all. And Dorothy and Joyce did their usual Laurel and Hardy imitation. And Billy Hughes, the beeman, told some of his jokes that only Frank and he find funny. And as usual Rita, Rita Cairns, sang "Oft in the Stilly Night," her party piece. That was my father's song, too. She has a sweet voice, really a child's voice, and she sings it beautifully. And as usual, when she had finished, so she tells me, she nodded her head and smiled and cried all at the same time.

And shortly after midnight — long before I had the brainwave to phone Mr. Rice — Tom McLaughlin, Tom the fiddler, played "The Lament for Limerick"! He played it softly, delicately. And suddenly, suddenly I felt utterly desolate. Maybe it was Rita singing "Oft in the Stilly Night" earlier. Or maybe it was because all that night nobody once mentioned the next day or how they thought the operation might go; and because nothing was said, maybe that made the occasion a bit unreal, a bit frantic. Or maybe it was because I was afraid that if things turned out as Frank and Mr. Rice hoped, I was afraid that I would never again know these people as I knew them now, with my own special knowledge of each of them, the distinctive sense each of them exuded for me; and knowing them differently, experiencing them differently, I wondered — I wondered would I ever be as close to them as I was now.

And then with sudden anger I thought: why am I going for this operation? None of this is my choosing. Then why is this happening to me? I am being used. Of course I trust Frank. Of course I trust Mr. Rice. But how can they know what they are taking away from me? How do they know what they are offering me? They don't. They can't. And have I anything to gain? — anything? — anything?

And then I knew, suddenly I knew why I was so desolate. It was the dread of exile, of being sent away. It was the desolation of homesickness.

And then a strange thing happened. As soon as Tom played the last note of "The Lament for Limerick," I found myself on my feet in the middle of the sitting-room and calling, "A hornpipe, Tom! A mad, fast hornpipe!" And the moment he began to play, I shouted — screamed, "Now watch me! Just you watch me!" And in a rage of anger and defiance I danced a wild and furious dance round and round that room; then out to the hall; then round the kitchen; then back to the room again and round it a third time. Mad and wild and frenzied. But so adroit, so efficient. No timidity, no hesitations, no falterings. Not a glass overturned, not a shoulder brushed. Weaving between all those people, darting between chairs and stools and cushions and bottles and glasses with complete assurance, with absolute confidence. Until Frank said something to Tom and stopped him playing.

God knows how I didn't kill myself or injure somebody. Or indeed how long it lasted. But it must have been terrifying to watch because, when I stopped, the room was hushed.

Frank whispered something to me. I don't know what he said — I was suddenly lost and anxious and frightened. I remember calling, "Rita? Where are you, Rita?" "Here at the window," she said. And I stumbled, groped my way to her and sat beside her. "Come on, sweetie," she said. "We'll have none of that. You're not allowed to cry. I'm the only one that's allowed to give a performance and then cry."

MR. RICE. The night before I operated on Molly Sweeney I thought about that high summer in my thirty-second year. Cairo. Another lecture; another conference; another posh hotel. As usual we all met up: Roger Bloomstein from New York, Hans Girder from Berlin, Hiroshi Matoba from Kyoto; myself. The meteors. The young turks. The four horsemen. Oslo last month. Helsinki next week. Paris the week after. That luminous, resplendent life. Those glowing, soaring careers.

Maria left the children with her parents in Geneva and flew down to join us. Still wan and translucent after the birth of Helga. And so beautiful; my God, so beautiful. We had a dinner party for her the night she arrived. Roger was master-of-ceremonies. Toasted her with his usual elegance. Said she was our Venus — no, our Galataea. She smiled her secret smile and said each of us was her Icarus.

Insatiable years. Work. Airports. Dinners. Laughter. Operating theatres. Conferences. Gossip. Publications. The professional jealousies and the necessary vigilance. The relentless, devouring excitement. But above all, above all the hunger to accomplish, the greed for achievement.

Shards of those memories came back to me on the night before I operated on Molly Sweeney on Tuesday, October the 7th. I had had a few drinks. I had had a lot of drinks. The fire was dead. I was drifting in and out of sleep.

Then the phone rang; an anxious sound at two in the morning. By the time I had pulled myself together and got to it, it had stopped. Wrong number probably.

I had another drink and sat beside the dead fire and relived for the hundredth time that other phone call. The small hours of the morning, too. In Cairo. That high summer of my thirty-second year.

It was Roger Bloomstein. Brilliant Roger. Treacherous Icarus. To tell me that Maria and he were at the airport and about to step on a plane for New York. They were deeply in love. They would be in touch in a few days. He was very sorry to have to tell me this. He hoped that in time I would see the situation from their point of view and come to understand it. And he hung up.

The mind was instantly paralysed. All I could think was: He's confusing seeing with understanding. Come on, Bloomstein. What's the matter with you? Seeing isn't understanding.

You know that! Don't talk rubbish, man!

And then ... and then ... oh, Jesus, Maria ...

FRANK.   Just as I was about to step into bed that night — that same Tuesday night that Dick Winterman phoned — the night of the operation — I was on the point of stepping into bed when suddenly, suddenly I remembered: Ethiopia is Abyssinia! Abyssinia is Ethiopia! They're the same place! Ethiopia is the new name for the old Abyssinia! For God's sake only last year the National Geographic Magazine had a brilliant article on it with all these stunning photographs. For God's sake I could write a book about Ethiopia! Absolutely *the* most interesting country in the world!

But of course I had to say no to Dick. As I said. Those rambling days were over. Molly was about to inherit a new world; and I had a sense — stupid, I know — I had a sense that maybe I was, too.

Pity to miss Abyssinia all the same — the one place in the whole world I've always dreamed of visiting; a phantom desire, a fantasy in the head. Pity to miss that.

You shouldn't have dangled it in front of me, Dick Winterman. Bloody, bloody heartbreaking.

MOLLY.   I remember so well the first day Frank came to the health club. That was the first time I'd met him. I was on a coffee-break. A Friday afternoon.

I had known of him for years of course. Rita Cairns and his friend Billy Hughes used to go out occasionally and I'd hear his name mentioned. She never said anything bad about him; but when his name came up, you got the feeling he was a bit ... different.

Anyhow that Friday he came into the club and Rita introduced us and we chatted. And for the whole ten minutes of my coffee-break he gave me a talk about a feasibility study he was doing on the blueback salmon, known in Oregon as sockeye and in Alaska as redfish, and of his plan to introduce it to Irish salmon farmers because it has the lowest wastage rate in all canning factories where it is used.

When he left I said to Rita that I'd never met a more enthusiastic man in my life. And Rita said in her laconic way, "Sweetie, who wants their enthusiasm focused on bluebacks for God's sake?"

Anyhow, ten minutes after he left, the phone rang. Could we meet that evening? Saturday? Sunday? What about a walk, a meal, a concert? Just a chat?

I asked him to call me the following Friday.

I thought a lot about him that week. I suppose he was the first man I really knew — apart from my father. And I liked his energy. I liked his enthusiasm. I liked his passion. Maybe what I really liked about him was that he was everything my father wasn't.

FRANK.   I spent the week in the library — the week after I first met her — one full week immersing myself in books and encyclopedias and magazines and articles — anything, everything I could find about eyes and vision and eye-diseases and blindness.

Fascinating. I can't tell you — fascinating.

I look out of my bedroom window and at a single glance I see the front garden and the road beyond and cars and buses and the tennis-courts on the far side and people playing on them and the hills beyond that. Everything — all those details and dozens more — all seen in one immediate, comprehensive perception. But Molly's world isn't perceived instantly, comprehensively. She composes a world from a sequence of impressions; one after the other; in time. For example she knows that this is a carving knife because first she can feel the handle; then she can feel this long blade; then this sharp edge. In sequence. In time. What is this object? These are ears. This is a furry body. Those are paws. That is a long tail. Ah, a cat! In sequence. Sequentially.

Right? Right. Now a personal question. You are going to ask this blind lady out for an evening. What would be the ideal entertainment for somebody like her? A meal? A concert? A walk? Maybe a swim? Billy Hughes says she's a wonderful swimmer. *(He shakes his head slowly.)*

The week in the library pays off. Know the answer instantly. Dancing. Take her dancing. With her disability the perfect, the absolute perfect relaxation. Forget about space, distance, who's close, who's far, who's approaching. Forget about time. This is not a sequence of events. This is one continuous, delightful event. Nothing leads to nothing else. There is only now. There is nothing subsequent. I am your eyes, your ears, your location, your sense of space. Trust me.

Dancing. Obvious.

Straight into a phone-box and asked her would she come with me to the Hikers Club dance the following Saturday. It'll be small, I said; more like a party. What do you say?

Silence.

We'll ask Billy and Rita and we'll make it a foursome and we'll have our own table and our own fun.

Not a word.

Please, Molly.

In my heart of hearts I really didn't think she'd say

yes. For God's sake why should she? Middle-aged. No skill. No job. No prospect of a job. Two rooms above Kelly's cake shop. And not exactly Rudolph Valentino. And when she did speak, when she said very politely, "Thank you, Frank. I'd love to go," do you know what I said? "Alright then." Bloody brilliant!

But I vowed to myself in that phone-box, I made a vow there and then that at the dance on Saturday night I wouldn't open the big mouth — big? — enormous for Christ's sake! — I wouldn't open it once all night, all week.

Talking of Valentino, in point of fact Valentino was no Adonis himself. Average height; average looks; mediocre talent. And if he hadn't died so young — in 1926 — he was only 31 — and in those mysterious circumstances that were never fully explained — he would never have become the cult figure the studios worked so hard to ...

Anyhow ...

MOLLY.   As usual Rita was wonderful. She washed my hair, my bloody useless hair — I can do nothing with it — she washed it in this special shampoo she concocted herself. Then she pulled it all away back from my face and piled it up just here and held it in place with her mother's silver ornamental comb. And she gave me her black shoes and her new woolen dress she'd just bought for her brother's wedding.

"There's still something not right," she said. "You still remind me of my Aunt Madge. Here — try these." And she whipped off her earrings and put them on me. "Now we have it," she said. "Bloody lethal. Francis Constantine, you're a dead duck!"

FRANK.   She had the time of her life. Knew she would. We danced every dance. Sang every song at the top of our voices. Ate an enormous supper. Even won a spot-prize: a tin of shortbread and a bottle of Albanian wine. The samba, actually. I wasn't bad at the samba once.

Dancing. I knew. I explained the whole thing to her. She had to agree. For God's sake she didn't have to say a word — she just glowed.

MOLLY.   It was almost at the end of the night — we were doing an old-time waltz — and suddenly he said to me, "You are such a beautiful woman, Molly."

Nobody had ever said anything like that to me before. I was afraid I might cry. And before I could say a word, he plunged on: "Of course I know that the very idea of appearance, of how things look, can't have much meaning for you. I do understand that. And maybe at heart you're a real philosophical skeptic because you question not only the idea of appearance but probably the existence of external reality itself. Do you, Molly?"

Honest to God ... the second last dance at the Hikers Club ... a leisurely old-time waltz ...

And I knew that night that he would ask me to marry him. Because he liked me — I knew he did. And because of my blindness — oh, yes, that fascinated him. He couldn't resist the different, the strange. I think he believed that some elusive off-beat truth resided in the quirky, the off-beat. I suppose that's what made him such a restless man. Rita of course said it was inevitable he would propose to me. "All part of the same pattern, sweetie: bees — whales — Iranian goats — Molly Sweeney."

Maybe she was right.

And I knew, too, after that night at the Hikers Club, that if he did ask me to marry him, for no very good reason at all I would probably say yes.

MR. RICE.   The morning of the operation I stood at the window of my office and watched them walk up the hospital drive. It was a blustery morning, threatening rain.

She didn't have her cane and she didn't hold his arm. But she moved briskly with her usual confidence; her head high; her face alert and eager. In her right hand she carried a grey, overnight bag.

He was on her left. Now in the open air a smaller presence in a shabby raincoat and cap; his hands clasped behind his back; his eyes on the ground; his head bowed slightly against the wind so that he looked ... passive. Not a trace of the assurance, the ebullience, that relentless energy.

And I thought: are they really such an unlikely couple? And I wondered what hopes moved in them as they came towards me. Were they modest? Reasonable? Outrageous? Of course, of course they were outrageous.

And suddenly and passionately and with utter selflessness I wanted nothing more in the world than that *their* inordinate hopes would be fulfilled, that I could give them their miracle. And I whispered to Hans Girder and to Matoba and to Murnahan and to Bloomstein — yes, to Bloomstein, too! — to gather round me this morning and steady my unsteady hand and endow me with all their exquisite skills.

Because as I watched them approach the hospital that blustery morning, one head alert, one head bowed, I was suddenly full of anxiety for both of them. Because I was afraid — even though she was in the hands of the best team in the whole world to deliver her miracle, because she was in the hands of the best team in the whole world — I was fearful, I suddenly knew that that courageous woman had everything, everything to lose.

INTERVAL

ACT TWO

MOLLY.   The morning the bandages were to be removed a staff nurse spent half-an-hour preparing me for Mr. Rice. It wasn't really her job, she told me, but this was my big day and I had to look my best and she was happy to do it.

So she sponged my face and hands. She made me clean my teeth again. She wondered did I use lipstick — maybe just for today? She did the best she could with my hair, God help her. She looked at my fingernails and suggested that a touch of clear varnish would be nice. She straightened the bow at the front of my night-dress and adjusted the collar of my dressing-gown. She put a dab of her own very special perfume on each of my wrists — she got it from a cousin in Paris. Then she stood back and surveyed me and said,

"Now. That's better. You'll find that from now on — if everything goes well of course — you'll find that you'll become very aware of your appearance. They all do for some reason. Don't be nervous. You look just lovely. He'll be here any minute now." I asked her where the bathroom was.

"At the end of the corridor. Last door on the right. I'll bring you."

"No," I said. "I'll find it."

I didn't need to go to the bathroom. I just wanted to take perhaps a last walk; in my own world; by myself.

I don't know what I expected when the bandages would be removed. I think maybe I didn't allow myself any expectations. I knew that in his heart Frank believed that somehow, miraculously, I would be given the perfect vision that sighted people have, even though Mr. Rice had told us again and again that my eyes weren't capable of that vision. And I knew what Mr. Rice hoped for: that I would have partial sight. "That would be a total success for me" is what he said. But I'm sure he meant it would be great for all of us.

As for myself, if I had any hope, I suppose it was that neither Frank nor Mr. Rice would be too disappointed because it had all become so important for them.

No, that's not accurate either. Yes, I did want to see. For God's sake of course I wanted to see. But that wasn't an expectation, not even a mad hope. If there was a phantom desire, a fantasy in my head, it was this. That perhaps by some means I might be afforded a brief excursion to this land of vision; not to live there — just to visit. And during my stay to devour it again and again and again with greedy, ravenous eyes. To gorge on all those luminous sights and wonderful spectacles until I knew every detail intimately and utterly — every ocean, every leaf, every field, every star, every tiny flower. And then, oh yes then to return home to my own world with all that rare understanding within me forever.

No, that wasn't even a phantom desire. Just a stupid fantasy. And it came into my head again when that poor nurse was trying to prettify me for Mr. Rice. And I thought to myself: it's like being back at school — I'm getting dressed up for the annual excursion.

When Mr. Rice did arrive, even before he touched me, I knew by his quick, shallow breathing that he was far more nervous than I was. And then as he took off the bandages his hands trembled and fumbled.

"There we are," he said. "All off. How does that feel?"

"Fine," I said. Even though I felt nothing. Were all the bandages off?

"Now, Molly. In your own time. Tell me what you see." Nothing. Nothing at all. Then out of the void a blur; a haze; a body of mist; a confusion of light, colour, movement. It had no meaning.

"Well?" he said. "Anything? Anything at all?"

I thought: don't panic; a voice comes from a face; that blur is his face; look at him.

"Well? Anything?"

Something moving; large, white; the nurse? And lines, black lines, vertical lines. The bed? The door?

"Anything, Molly?" A bright light that hurt. The window maybe?

"I'm holding my hand before your eyes, Molly. Can you see it?"

A reddish blob in front of my face; rotating; liquefying; pulsating. Keep calm. Concentrate.

"Can you see my hand, Molly?"

"I think so ... I'm not sure ..."

"Now I'm moving my hand slowly."

"Yes ... yes ..."

"Do you see my hand moving?"

"Yes ..."

"What way is it moving?"

"Yes ... I do see it ... up and down ... up and down.... Yes! I see it! I do! Yes! Moving up and down! Yes-yes-yes!"

"Splendid!" he said. "Absolutely splendid! You are a clever lady!"

And there was such delight in his voice. And my head was suddenly giddy. And I thought for a moment — for a moment I thought I was going to faint.

FRANK.   There was some mix-up about what time the bandages were to be removed. At least I was confused. For some reason I got it into my head that they were to be taken off at eight in the morning, October the 8th, the day after the operation. A Wednesday, I remember, because I was doing a crash-course in speed-reading and I had to switch from the morning to the afternoon class for that day.

So; eight o'clock sharp; there I was sitting in the hospital, all dickied up — the good suit, the shoes polished, the clean shirt, the new tie, and with my bunch of flowers, waiting to be summoned to Molly's ward.

The call finally did come — at a quarter to twelve. Ward 10. Room 17. And of course by then I knew the operation was a disaster.

Knocked. Went in. Rice was there. And a staff nurse, a tiny little woman. And an Indian man — the anaesthetist, I think. The moment I entered he rushed out without saying a word.

And Molly. Sitting very straight in a white chair beside her bed. Her hair pulled away back from her face and piled up just here. Wearing a lime-green dressing-gown that Rita Cairns had lent her and the blue slippers I got her for her last birthday.

There was a small bruise mark below her right eye. I thought: how young she looks, and so beautiful, so very beautiful.

"There she is," said Rice. "How does she look?"

"She looks well."

"Well? She looks wonderful! And why not? Everything went brilliantly! A complete success! A dream!"

He was so excited, there was no trace of the posh accent. And he bounced up and down on the balls of his feet. And he took my hand and shook it as if he were congratulating me. And the tiny staff nurse laughed and said "Brilliant! Brilliant!" and in her excitement knocked the chart off the end of the bed and then laughed even more.

"Speak to her!" said Rice. "Say something!"

"How are you?" I said to Molly.

"How do I look?"

"*You look great.*"

"Do you like my black eye?"

"I didn't notice it," I said.

"I'm feeling great," she said. "Really. But what about you?"

"What do you mean?"

"Did you manage alright on your own last night?"

I suppose at that moment and in those circumstances it did sound a bit funny. Anyhow Rice laughed out loud and of course the staff nurse; and then Molly and I had to laugh, too. In relief, I suppose, really ...

Then Rice said to me,

"Aren't you going to give the lady her flowers?"

"Sorry," I said. "I got Rita to choose them. She said they're your favourite." Could she see them? I didn't know what to do. Should I take her hand and put the flowers into it? I held them in front of her. She reached out confidently and took them from me.

"They're lovely," she said. "Thank you. Lovely."

And she held them at arms length, directly in front of her face, and turned them round. Suddenly Rice said,

"What colour are they, Molly?" She didn't hesitate at all.

"They're blue," she said. "Aren't they blue?"

"They certainly are! And the paper?" Rice asked. "What colour is the wrapping paper?"

"Is it ... yellow?"

"Yes! So you know some colours! Excellent! Really excellent!" And the staff nurse clapped with delight.

"Now — a really hard question, and I'm not sure I know the answer to it myself. What sort of flowers are they?"

She brought them right up to her face. She turned them upside down. She held them at arm's length again. She stared at them — peered at them really — for what seemed an age. I knew how anxious she was by the way her mouth was working.

"Well, Molly? Do you know what they are?"

We waited. Another long silence. Then suddenly she closed her eyes shut tight. She brought the flowers right up against her face and inhaled in quick gulps and at the same time, with her free hand, swiftly, deftly felt the stems and the leaves and the blossoms. Then with her eyes still shut tight she called out desperately, defiantly,

"They're cornflowers! That's what they are! Cornflowers! Blue cornflowers! Centaurea!"

Then for maybe half-a-minute she cried. Sobbed really.

The staff nurse looked uneasily at Rice. He held up his hand.

"Cornflowers, indeed. Splendid," he said very softly. "Excellent. It has been a heady day. But we're really on our way now, aren't we?"

I went back to the hospital again that night after my class. She was in buoyant form. I never saw her so animated.

"I can see, Frank!" she kept saying. "Do you hear me? — I can see!" Mr. Rice was a genius! Wasn't it all wonderful? The nurses were angels! Wasn't I thrilled? She loved my red tie — it was red, wasn't it? And everybody was so kind. Dorothy and Joyce brought those chocolates during their lunchbreak. And old Mr. O'Neill sent that get well card — there — look — on the window sill. And didn't the flowers look beautiful in that pink vase? She would have the operation on the left eye just as soon as Mr. Rice would agree. And then, Frank, and then and then and then and then — oh, God, what then!

I was so happy, so happy for her. Couldn't have been happier for God's sake.

But just as on that first morning in Rice's bungalow when the only thing my mind could focus on was the smell of fresh whiskey off his breath, now, all I could think of was some ... some ... some absurd scrap of information a Norwegian fisherman told me about the eyes of whales.

Whales for God's sake!

Stupid information. Useless, off-beat information. Stupid, useless, quirky mind ...

Molly was still in full flight when a nurse came in and said that visiting time was long over and that Mrs. Sweeney needed all her strength to face tomorrow.

"How do I look?"

"Great," I said.

"Really, Frank?"

"Honestly. Wonderful."

"Black eye and all?"

"You wouldn't notice it," I said. She caught my hand.

"Do you think...?"

"Do I think what?"

"Do you think I look pretty, Frank?"

"You look beautiful," I said. "Just beautiful."

"Thank you."

I kissed her on the forehead and as I said good night to her, she gazed intently at my face as if she were trying to read it. Her eyes were bright; unnaturally bright; burnished. And her expression was open and joyous. But as I said good night I had the feeling she wasn't as joyous as she looked.

MR. RICE.   When I look back over my working life I suppose I must have done thousands of operations. Sorry — performed. Bloomstein always corrected me on that: "Come on, you bloody bogman! We're not mechanics. We're artists. We perform." *(He shrugs his shoulders in dismissal.)*

And of those thousands I wonder how many I'll remember.

I'll remember Ballybeg. Of course I'll remember Ballybeg. And the courageous Molly Sweeney. And I'll remember it not because of the operation — the operation wasn't all that complex; nor because the circumstances were special; nor indeed because a woman who had been blind for over forty years got her sight back. Yes, yes, yes, I'll remember it for all those reasons. Of course I will. But the core, the very heart of the memory will be something different, something altogether different.

Perhaps I should explain that after that high summer of my thirty-second year — that episode in Cairo — the dinner party for Maria — Bloomstein's phone call — all that tawdry drama — my life no longer ... cohered. I withdrew from medicine, from friendships, from all the consolations of work and the familiar; and for seven years and seven months — sounds like a fairy tale I used to read to Aisling — I subsided into a terrible darkness ...

But I was talking of Molly's operation and my memory of that. And the core of that memory is this. That for seventy-five minutes in the theatre on that blustery October morning, the darkness miraculously lifted, and I performed — I watched myself do it — I performed so assuredly and with such skill, so elegantly, so efficiently, so economically — yes, yes, yes, of course it sounds vain — vanity has nothing to do with it — but suddenly, miraculously all the gifts, all the gifts were mine again, abundantly mine, joyously mine; and on that blustery

39

October morning I had such a feeling of mastery and — how can I put it? — such a sense of playfulness for God's sake that I knew I was restored. No, no, no, not fully restored. Never fully restored. But a sense that a practical restoration, perhaps a restoration to something truer — that was possible. Yes, maybe that was possible ...

Yes, I'll remember Ballybeg. And when I left that dreary little place, that's the memory I took away with me. The place where I restored her sight to Molly Sweeney. Where the terrible darkness lifted. Where the shaft of light glanced off me again.

MOLLY. Mr. Rice said he couldn't have been more pleased with my progress. He called me his Miracle Molly. I liked him a lot more as the weeks passed.

And as usual Rita was wonderful. She let me off work early every Monday, Wednesday and Friday. And I'd dress up in this new coat I'd bought — a mad splurge to keep the spirits up — brilliant scarlet with a matching beret — Rita said I could be seen from miles away, like a distress signal — anyhow in all my new style I'd walk to the hospital on those three afternoons — without my cane! — and sometimes that was scary, I can tell you. And Mr. Rice would examine me and say, "Splendid, Molly, Splendid!" And then he'd pass me on to a psychotherapist, Mrs. O'Connor, a beautiful looking woman according to Frank, and I'd do all sorts of tests with her. And then she'd pass me on to George, her husband, for more tests — he was a behavioural psychologist, if you don't mind, a real genius apparently — the pair of them were writing a book on me. And then I'd go back to Mr. Rice again and he'd say "Splendid!" again. And then I'd walk home — still no cane! — and have Frank's tea waiting for him when he'd get back from the library.

I can't tell you how kind Frank was to me, how patient he was. As soon as tea was over, he'd sit at the top of the table and he'd put me at the bottom and he'd begin my lessons.

He'd put something in front of me — maybe a bowl of fruit — and he'd say,

"What have I got in my hand?"

"A piece of fruit."

"What sort of fruit?"

"An orange, Frank. I know the colour, don't I?"

"Very clever. Now, what's this?"

"It's a pear."

"You're guessing."

"Let me touch it."

"Not allowed. You already have your tactile engrams. We've got to build up a repertory of visual engrams to connect with them."

And I'd say, "For God's sake stop showing off your posh new words, Frank. It's a banana."

"Sorry. Try again."

"It's a peach. Right?"

"Splendid!" he'd say in Mr. Rice's accent. "It certainly is a peach. Now, what's this?"

And he'd move on to knives and forks, or shoes and slippers, or all the bits and pieces on the mantelpiece for maybe another hour or more. Every night. Seven nights a week.

Oh, yes, Frank couldn't have been kinder to me.

Rita, too. Even kinder. Even more patient.

And all my customers at the health club, the ones who had massages regularly, they sent me a huge bouquet of pink-and-white tulips. And the club I used to swim with, they sent me a beautiful gardening book. God knows what they thought — that I'd now be able to pick it up and read it? But everyone was great, just great.

Oh, yes, I lived in a very exciting world for those first weeks after the operation. Not at all like that silly world I wanted to visit and devour — none of that nonsense.

No, the world that I now saw — half-saw, peered at really — it was a world of wonder and surprise and delight. Oh, yes; wonderful, surprising, delightful. And joy — such joy — small unexpected joys that came in such profusion and passed so quickly that there was never enough time to savour them.

But it was a very foreign world, too. And disquieting; even alarming. Every colour dazzled. Every light blazed. Every shape an apparition, a spectre that appeared suddenly from nowhere and challenged you. And all that movement — nothing ever still — everything in motion all the time; and every movement unexpected, somehow threatening. Even the sudden sparrows in the garden, they seemed aggressive, dangerous.

So that after a time the mind could absorb no more sensation. Just one more colour — light — movement — ghostly shape — and suddenly the head imploded and the hands shook and the heart melted with panic. And the only escape — the only way to live — was to sit absolutely still; and shut the eyes tight; and immerse yourself in darkness; and wait. Then when the hands were still and the heart quiet, slowly open the eyes again. And emerge. And try to find the courage to face it all once more.

I tried to explain to Frank once how — I suppose how terrifying it all was. But naturally, naturally he was far more concerned with teaching me practical things. And one day when I mentioned to Mr. Rice that I didn't think I'd find things as unnerving as I did, he said in a very icy voice, "And what sort of world did you expect, Mrs. Sweeney?"

Yes, it was a strange time. An exciting time, too — oh, yes, exciting. But so strange. And during those weeks after the operation I found myself thinking more and more about my mother and father, but especially about my mother and what it must have been like for her living in that huge, echoing house.

MR. RICE.   I operated on the second eye, the left eye, six weeks after the first operation. I had hoped it might have been a healthier eye. But when the cataract was removed, we found a retina much the same as in the right: traces of pigmentosa, scarred macula, areas atrophied. However with both eyes functioning to some degree her visual field was larger and she fixated better. She could now see from a medical point of view. From a psychological point of view she was still blind. In other words she now had to learn to see.

FRANK.   As we got closer to the end of that year, it was quite clear that Molly was changing — had changed. One of the most fascinating insights into the state of her mind at that time was given to me by Jean O'Connor, the psychotherapist; very interesting woman; brilliant actually; married to George, a behavioural psychologist, a second-rater if you ask me; and what a bore — what a bore! Do you know what that man did? Lectured me one day for over an hour on cheese making if you don't mind. Anyhow — anyhow — the two of them — the O'Connors — they were doing this book on Molly; a sort of documentation of her 'case history' from early sight to life-long blindness to sight restored to ... whatever. And the way Jean explained Molly's condition to me was this.

All of us live on a swing, she said. And the swing normally moves smoothly and evenly across a narrow range of the usual emotions. Then we have a crisis in our life so that instead of moving evenly from, say, feeling sort of happy to feeling sort of miserable, we now swing from elation to despair, from unimaginable delight to utter wretchedness. The word she used was 'delivered' to show how passive we are in this terrifying game: we are delivered into one emotional state — snatched away from it — delivered into the opposite emotional state. And we can't help ourselves. We can't escape. Until eventually we can endure no more abuse — become incapable of experiencing anything, feeling anything at all.

That's how Jean O'Connor explained Molly's behaviour to me. Very interesting woman. Brilliant actually. And beautiful, too. Oh, yes, all the gifts. And what she said helped me to understand Molly's extraordinary behaviour — difficult behaviour — yes, goddammit very difficult behaviour over those weeks leading up to Christmas.

For example — for example. One day, out of the blue, a Friday evening, in December, five o'clock, I'm about to go to the Hikers Club, and she says, "I feel like a swim, Frank. Let's go for a swim now." At this stage I'm beginning to recognise the symptoms: the defiant smile, the excessive enthusiasm; some reckless, dangerous proposal. Fine. Fine, I say. Even though it's pitch dark and raining.

So we'll go to the swimming-pool? Oh, no. She wants to swim in the sea. And not only swim in the sea on a wet Friday night in December, but she wants to go out to the rocks at the far end of Tramore and she wants to climb up on top of Napoleon Rock as we call it locally — it's the highest rock there, a cliff really — and I'm to tell her if the tide is in or out and how close are the small rocks in the sea below and how deep the water is because she's going to dive — to dive for God's sake — the eighty feet from the top of Napoleon down into the Atlantic ocean. "And why not, Frank? Why not for God's sake?"

Oh, yes, an enormous change. Something extraordinary about all that. Then there was the night I watched her through the bedroom door. She was sitting at her dressing-table, in front of the mirror, trying her hair in different ways. When she would have it in a certain way, she'd lean close to the mirror and peer into it and turn her head from side to side. But you knew she couldn't read her reflection, could scarcely even see it. Then she would try the hair in a different style and she'd lean into the mirror again until her face was almost touching it and again she'd turn first to one side and then the other. And you knew that all she saw was a blur.

Then after about half-a-dozen attempts she stood up and came to the door — it was then I could see she was crying — and she switched off the light. Then she went back to the dressing-table and sat down again; in the dark; for maybe an hour; sat there and gazed listlessly at the black mirror.

Yes, she did dive into the Atlantic from the top of Napoleon Rock that Friday night in December. First time in her life. Difficult times. Oh, I can't tell you. Difficult times for all of us.

MR. RICE.   The dangerous period for Molly came — as it does for all patients — when the first delight and excitement at having vision have died away. The old world with its routines, all the consolations of work and the familiar, is gone forever. A sighted world — a partially sighted world, for that is the best it will ever be — is available. But to compose it, to put it together, demands effort and concentration and patience that are almost super-human.

So the question she had to ask herself was: how much do I want this world? And am I prepared to make that enormous effort to get it?

FRANK.   Then there was a new development — as if she hadn't enough troubles already. A frightening new development. She began getting spells of dizziness when everything seemed in a thick fog, all external reality became just a haze. This would hit her for no reason at all — at work, or walking home, or in the house; and it would last for an hour, maybe several hours.

Rice had no explanation for it. But you could see he was concerned.

"It's called gnosis," he said.

"How do you spell that?"

"G-n-o-s-i-s."

"And what is it?"

"It's a condition of impaired vision, Mr. Sweeney." He really was a right little bastard at times.

Anyhow, I looked it up in the library, and interestingly, interestingly I could find no reference at all to a medical condition called 'gnosis.' But according to the dictionary the word meant a mystical knowledge, a knowledge of spiritual things! And my first thought was: Good old Molly! Molly's full of mystical knowledge! — God forgive me; I really didn't mean to be so cheap.

I meant to tell Rice about *that* meaning of the word the next time I met him — just to bring him down a peg. But it slipped my mind. I suppose because the condition disappeared as suddenly as it appeared. And anyway she had so many troubles at the stage that my skirmishes with Rice didn't matter any more.

MOLLY. Tests — tests — tests — tests — tests! Between Mr. Rice and Jean O'Connor and George O'Connor and indeed Frank himself I must have spent months and months being analysed and answering questions and identifying drawings and making sketches. And, God, those damned tests with photographs and lights and objects — those endless tricks and illusions and distortions — the Zöllner Illusion, the Ames Distorting Room, the Staircase Illusion, the Müller-Lyer Illusion. And they never told you if you had passed or failed so you always assumed you failed. Such peace — such peace when they were all finished.

    I stopped at the florist one evening to get something for Tony and Betty from this side — what was this side; Molly's father and mother. For their wedding anniversary. And I spotted this little pot of flowers, like large buttercups, about six inches tall, with blue petals and what seemed to me a whitish centre. I thought I recognised them but I wasn't quite sure. And I wouldn't allow myself to touch them.

    "I'll take these," I said to the man.

    "Pretty, aren't they?" he said, "Just in from Holland this morning. And do you know what? — I can't remember what they're called. Do you know?"

    "They're nemophila."

    "Are they?"

    "Yes," I said. "Feel the leaves. They should be dry and feathery."

    "You're right," he said. "That's what they are. They have another name, haven't they?"

    "Baby Blue Eyes," I said.

    "That's it! I'd forgotten that! Getting too old for this job."

    Yes, that gave me some pleasure. One silly little victory. And when I took them home and held them up to my face and looked closely at them, they weren't nearly as pretty as buttercups. Weren't pretty at all. Couldn't give that as a present next door.

FRANK.   It was the clever Jean O'Connor who spotted the distress signals first. She said to me: "We should be seeing a renaissance of personality at this point. Because if that doesn't take place — and it's not — then you can expect a withdrawal."

And she was right. That's what happened. Molly just ... withdrew.

Then in the middle of February she lost her job in the health club. And now Rita was no longer a friend. And that was so unfair — Rita kept making allowances for her long after any other boss would have got rid of her; turning in late; leaving early; maybe not even making an appearance for two or three days. Just sitting alone in her bedroom with her eyes shut, maybe listening to the radio, maybe just sitting there in silence.

I made a last effort on the first of March. I took her new scarlet coat out of the wardrobe and I said, "Come on, girl! Enough of this. We're going for a long walk on Tramore beach. Then we'll have a drink at Moriarity's. Then we'll have dinner in that new Chinese place. Right? Right!" And I left the coat at the foot of her bed.

And that's where it lay for weeks. And weeks. In fact she never wore it out again.

And at that point I had come to the end of my tether. There seemed to be nothing more I could do.

MR. RICE.   In those last few months a new condition appeared. She began showing symptoms of a condition known as blindsight. This is a physiological condition, not psychological. On those occasions she claimed she could see nothing, absolutely nothing at all. And indeed she was telling the truth. But even as she said this, she behaved as if she could see — reach for her purse, avoid a chair that was in her way, lift a book and hand it to you. She *was* indeed receiving visual signals and she *was* indeed responding to them. But because of a malfunction in part of the cerebral cortex none of this perception reached her consciousness. She was totally unconscious of seeing anything at all.

In other words she *had* vision — but vision that was utterly useless to her.

Blindsight ... curious word ...

I remember in Cleveland once Bloomstein and Maria and I were in a restaurant and when Maria left the table Bloomstein said to me,

"Beautiful lady. You *do* know that?"

"I know," I said.

"Do you really?"

I said of course I did.

"That's not how you behave," he said. "You behave like a man with blindsight."

FRANK.   We were in the pub this night, Billy Hughes and myself, and this man comes up to me in the bar, says he's a journalist from a Dublin paper, asks would I be interested in giving him the full story about Molly.

He seemed a decent man. I talked to him for maybe an hour at most. Of course it was stupid. And I really didn't do it for the bloody money.

Jack from next door spotted the piece and brought it in. "Miracle Cure False Dawn. Molly sulks in darkness. Husband drowns sorrow in pub."

Of course she heard about it — God knows how. And now I was as bad as all the others: I had let her down, too.

MOLLY.   During all those years when my mother was in the hospital with her nerves my father brought me to visit her only three times. Maybe that was her choice. Or his. I never knew.

But I have a vivid memory of each of those three visits.

One of the voice of a youngish woman. My father and mother are in her ward, surrounded by a screen, fighting as usual, and I'm standing outside in the huge echoey corridor.

And I can hear a young woman sobbing at the far end of the corridor. More lamenting than sobbing. And even though a lot of people are passing along that corridor I remember wondering why nobody paid any attention to her. And for some reason the sound of the lamentation stayed with me.

And I remember another patient, an old man, leaning over me and enveloping me in the smell of snuff. He slipped a coin into my hand and said, "Go out and buy us a fancy new car, son, and the two of us will drive away to beautiful Fethard-on-Sea." And he laughed. He had given me a shilling.

And the third memory is of my mother sitting on the side of her bed, shouting at my father, screaming at him, "She should be at a blind school! You know she should! But you know the real reason you won't send her? Not because you haven't the money. Because you want to punish me."

I didn't tell Mr. Rice that story when he first asked me about my childhood. Out of loyalty to father maybe. Maybe out of loyalty to mother, too.

Anyhow those memories came into my head the other day. I can't have been more than six or seven at the time.

MR. RICE.   In those last few months it was hard to recognise the woman who had first come to my house. The confident way she took my hand. Her calm and her independence. The way she held her head.

How self-sufficient she had been then — her home, her job, her friends, her swimming; so naturally, so easily experiencing her world with her hands alone.

And we had once asked so glibly: what has she to lose?

MOLLY.   In those last few months I was seeing less and less. I was living in the hospital then, mother's old hospital. And what was strange was that there were times when I didn't know if the things I did see were real or was I imagining them. I seemed to be living on a borderline between fantasy and reality.

Yes, that was a strange state. Anxious at first; oh, very anxious. Because it meant that I couldn't trust any more what sight I still had. It was no longer trust-worthy.

But as time went on that anxiety receded; seemed to be a silly anxiety. Not that I began trusting my eyes again. Just that trying to discriminate, to distinguish between what might be real and what might be imagined, being guided by what father used to call 'excellent testimony' — that didn't seem to matter all that much, seemed to matter less and less. And for some reason the less it mattered, the more I thought I could see.

MR. RICE.   In those last few months — she was living in the psychiatric hospital at that point — I knew I had lost contact with her. She had moved away from us all. She wasn't in her old blind world — she was exiled from that. And the sighted world, which she had never found hospitable, wasn't available to her any more.

My sense was that she was trying to compose another life that was neither sighted nor unsighted, somewhere she hoped was beyond disappointment; somewhere, she hoped, without expectation.

FRANK.   The last time I saw Rice was on the following Easter Sunday; April the 7th; six months to the day after the first operation. Fishing on the lake called Lough Anna away up in the hills. Billy Hughes spotted him first.

"Isn't that your friend, Mr. Rice? Wave to him, man!"

And what were Billy and I doing up there in the wilds? Embarrassing. But I'll explain.

Ballybeg got its water supply from Lough Anna and in the summer, when the lake was low, from two small adjoining lakes. So to make the supply more efficient it was decided that at the end of April the two small lakes would be emptied into Lough Anna and it would become the sole reservoir for the town. That would raise the water level of Anna by fifteen feet and of course ruin the trout fishing there — not that that worried them. So in fact that Easter Sunday would have been Rice's last time to fish there. But he probably knew that because Anna was his favourite lake; he was up there every chance he got; and he had told me once that he had thought of putting a boat on it. Anyhow — anyhow.

Billy Hughes and his crazy scheme. He had heard that there was a pair of badgers in a sett at the edge of the lake. When Anna was flooded in three weeks time, they would be drowned. They would have to be moved. Would I help him?

Move two badgers! Wonderful! So why did I go with him? Partly to humour the eejit. But really, I suppose, really because that would be our last day together, that Easter Sunday.

And that's how we spent it — digging two bloody badgers out of their sett. Dug for two-and-a-half-hours. Then flung old fishing nets over them to immobilise them. Then lifted them into two wheelbarrows. Then hauled those wheelbarrows along a sheep track up the side of the mountain. And then — listen to this — then tried to force them into an old, abandoned sett half-way up the mountain! Brilliant Billy Hughes!

Because of course the moment we cut them out of the nets and tried to push them down the new hole, well naturally they went wild; bit Billy's ankle and damn near fractured my arm; and then went careering down the hillside in a mad panic, trailing bits of net behind them. And because they can't see too well in the daylight or maybe because they're half-blind anyway, banging into rocks and bumping into each other and sliding and rolling and tumbling all over the place. And where did they head for? Of course — of course — straight back to the old sett at the edge of the water — the one we'd destroyed with all our digging!

Well, what could you do but laugh? Hands blistered, bleeding ankle, sore arm, filthy clothes. Flung ourselves on the heather and laughed until our sides hurt. And then Billy turned to me and said very formally, "Happy Easter, Frank" and it seemed the funniest thing in the world and off we went again. What an eejit that man was!

Rice joined us when we were putting the wheelbarrows into the back of Billy's van.

"I was watching you from the far side," he said. "What in God's name were you doing?"

Billy told him.

"Good heavens!" he said, posh as ever. "A splendid idea. Always a man for the noble pursuit, Frank."

The bastard couldn't resist it, I knew. But for some reason he didn't anger me that day; didn't even annoy me. Maybe because his fishing outfit was a couple of sizes too big for him and in those baggy trousers he looked a bit like a circus clown. Maybe because at that moment, after that fiasco with the badgers, standing on that shore that would be gone in a few weeks time, none of the three of us — Billy, Rice, myself — none of the three of us seemed such big shots at that moment. Or maybe he didn't annoy me that Easter Sunday afternoon because I knew I'd probably never see him again. I was heading off to Ethiopia in the morning.

We left the van outside Billy's flat and he walked me part of the way home.

When we got to the courthouse I said he'd come far enough: we'd part here. I hoped he'd get work. I hoped he'd meet some decent woman who'd marry him and beat some sense into him. And I'd be back home soon, very soon, the moment I sorted out the economy of Ethiopia ... the usual stuff.

Then we hugged quickly and he walked away and I looked after him and watched his straight back and the quirky way he threw out his left leg as he walked and I thought, my God, I thought how much I'm going to miss that bloody man.

And when he disappeared round the corner of the courthouse, I thought, too — I thought, too — Abyssinia for Christ's sake — or whatever it's called — Ethiopia — Abyssinia — whatever it's called — who cares what it's called — who gives a damn — who in his right mind wants to go there for Christ's sake? Not you. You certainly don't. Then why don't you stay where you are for Christ's sake? What are you looking for?

Oh, Jesus ...

MR. RICE.   Roger Bloomstein was killed in an air-crash on the evening of the Fourth of July. He was flying his plane from New York to Cape Cod where Maria and he had rented a house for the summer. An eye-witness said the engine stopped suddenly, and for a couple of seconds the plane seemed to sit suspended in the sky, golden and glittering in the setting sun, and then plummeted into the sea just south of Martha's Vineyard.

The body was never recovered.

I went to New York for the memorial service the following month. Hiroshi Matoba couldn't come: he had had a massive heart attack the previous week. So of the four horsemen, the brilliant meteors, there were only the two of us: Hans, now the internationally famous Herr Girder, silver-haired, sleek, smiling; and myself, seedy, I knew, after a bad flight and too much whiskey.

Girder asked about Molly. He had read an article George O'Connor had written about 'Mrs. M.' in the *Journal of Psychology*. The enquiry sounded casual but the smiling eyes couldn't conceal the vigilance. So the vigilance was still necessary despite the success, maybe more necessary because of the success.

"Lucky Paddy Rice," he said. "The chance of a lifetime. Fell on your feet again."

"Not as lucky as you, Hans."

"But it didn't end happily for the lady?"

" 'Fraid not," I said.

"Too bad. No happy endings. So she is totally sightless now?"

"Totally."

"And mentally?"

"Good days — bad days," I said.

"But she won't survive?"

"Who's to say?" I said.

"No, no. They don't survive. That's the pattern. But they'll insist on having the operation, won't they? And who's to dissuade them?"

"Let me get you a drink," I said and I walked away.

I watched Maria during the service. Her beauty had always been chameleon. She had an instinctive beauty for every occasion. And today with her drained face and her dazed eyes and that fragile body, today she was utterly vulnerable, and at the same time, within her devastation, wholly intact and untouchable. I had never seen her more beautiful.

When the service was over she came to me and thanked me for coming. We talked about Aisling and Helga. They were having a great time with her parents in Geneva; they loved it there and her parents spoiled them; they weren't good at answering letters but they liked getting mine even though they were a bit scrappy. They were happy girls, she said.

Neither of us spoke Roger's name.

Then she took my hand and kissed it and held it briefly against her cheek. It was a loving gesture. But for all its tenderness, because of its tenderness, I knew she was saying a final goodbye to me.

As soon as I got back to Ballybeg I resigned from the hospital and set about gathering whatever belongings I had. The bungalow was rented, never more than a lodging. So the moving out was simple — some clothes, a few books, the fishing rods. Pity to leave the lakes at that time of year. But the lake I enjoyed most — a lake I had grown to love — it had been destroyed by flooding. So it was all no great upheaval.

I called on Molly the night before I left. The nurse said she was very frail. But she could last forever or she could slip away tonight. "It's up to herself," she said. "But a lovely woman. No trouble at all. If they were all as nice and quiet ..."

She was sleeping and I didn't waken her. Propped up against the pillows; her mouth open; her breathing shallow; a scarlet coat draped around her shoulders; the wayward hair that had given her so much trouble now contained in a net.

And looking down at her I remembered — was it all less than a year ago? — I had a quick memory of the first time I saw her in my house, and the phantom desire, the insane fantasy that crossed my mind that day: was this the chance of a lifetime that might pull my life together, rescue a career, restore a reputation? Dear God, that opulent fantasy life ...

And looking down at her — the face relaxed, that wayward hair contained in a net — I thought how I had failed her. Of course I had failed her. But at least, at least for a short time she did see men 'walking as if like trees'. And I think, perhaps, yes I think she understood more than any of us what she did see.

MOLLY. When I first went to Mr. Rice I remember him asking me was I able to distinguish between light and dark and what direction light came from. And I remember thinking: oh my God, he's asking you profound questions about good and evil and about the source of knowledge and about big mystical issues! Careful! Don't make a fool of yourself! And of course all the poor man wanted to know was how much vision I had. And I could answer him easily now: I can't distinguish between light and dark, nor the direction from which light comes, and I certainly wouldn't see the shadow of Frank's hand in front of my face. Yes, that's all long gone. Even the world of touch has shrunk. No, not that it has shrunk; just that I seem to need much less of it now. And after all that anxiety and drudgery we went through with engrams and the need to establish connections between visual and tactile engrams and synchronising sensations of touch and sight and composing a whole new world. But I suppose all that had to be attempted.

I like this hospital. The staff are friendly. And I have loads of visitors. Tony and Betty and baby Molly from this side — well, what used to be this side. They light an odd fire in the house, too, to keep it aired for Frank. And Mary from that side. She hasn't told me yet but I'm afraid Jack has cleared off. And Billy Hughes; out of loyalty to Frank; every Sunday in life, God help me; God help *him*. And Rita. Of course, Rita. We never talk about the row we had. That's all in the past. I love her visits: she has all the gossip from the club. Next time she's here I must ask her to sing "Oft in the Stilly Night" for me. And no crying at the end!

And old Mr. O'Neill! Yes! Dan McGrew himself! He was looking just wonderful; not a day over forty. And he stood in the middle of the ward and did the whole thing for me — "A bunch of the boys were whooping it up in the Malamute saloon." Oh, that gave my heart a great lift.

And yesterday I got a letter, twenty-seven pages long. Frank — who else? It took the nurse an hour to read it to me. Ethiopia is paradise. The people are heroes. The climate is hell. The relief workers are completely dedicated. Never in his life has he felt so committed, so passionate, so fulfilled. And they have a special bee out there, the African bee, that produces twice as much honey as our bees and is immune to all known bee diseases and even though it has an aggressive nature he is convinced it would do particularly well in Ireland. And in his very limited spare time he has taken up philosophy. It is fascinating stuff. There is a man called Aristotle that he thinks highly of. I should read him, he says. And he sent a money order for two pounds and he'll write again soon.

Mother comes in occasionally; in her pale blue headscarf and muddy Wellingtons. Nobody pays much attention to her. She just wanders through the wards. She spent so much time here herself, I suppose she has an affection for the place. She doesn't talk much — she never did. But when she sits uneasily on the edge of my bed, as if she were waiting to be summoned, her face always frozen in that nervous half-smile, I think I know her better than I ever knew her and I begin to love her all over again.

Mr. Rice came to see me one night before he went away.

I was propped up in bed, drifting in and out of sleep, and he stood swaying at the side of the bed for maybe five minutes, just gazing at me, I kept my eyes closed. Then he took both my hands in his and said,

"I'm sorry, Molly Sweeney. I'm so sorry."

And off he went.

I suppose it was mean of me to pretend I was asleep.

But the smell of whiskey was suffocating; and the night nurse told me that on his way out the front door he almost fell down the stone steps.

And sometimes father drops in on his way from court. And we do imaginary tours of the walled garden and compete with each other in the number of flowers and shrubs each of us can identify. I asked him once why he had never sent me to a school for the blind. And as soon as I asked him I knew I sounded as if I was angry about it, as if I wanted to catch him out. But he wasn't at all disturbed. The answer was simple, he said. Mother wasn't well; and when she wasn't in hospital she needed my company at home. But even though I couldn't see the expression on his face, his voice was lying. The truth of the matter was he was always mean with money; he wouldn't pay the blind school fees.

And once — just once — I thought maybe I heard the youngish woman sobbing quietly at the far end of the corridor, more lamenting than sobbing. But I wasn't sure. And when I asked the nurse, she said I must have imagined it; there was nobody like that on our floor. And of course my little old snuff man must be dead years ago — the man who wanted to drive us to beautiful Fethard-on-Sea. He gave me a shilling, I remember; a lot of money in those days.

I think I see nothing at all now. But I'm not absolutely sure of that. Anyhow my borderline country is where I live now. I'm at home there. Well … at ease there. It certainly doesn't worry me any more that what I think I see may be fantasy or indeed what I take to be imagined may very well be real — what's Frank's term? — external reality. Real — imagined — fact — fiction — fantasy — reality — there it seems to be. And it seems to be alright. And why should I question any of it any more?

THE END

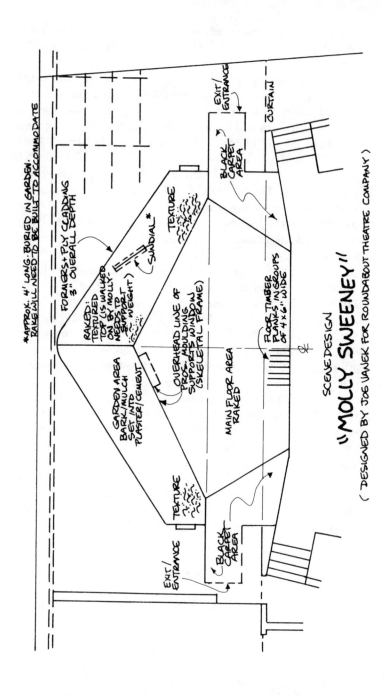

*APPROX. 4' LONG: BURIED IN GARDEN.
RAKE WILL NEED TO BE BUILT TO ACCOMMODATE

FORMERS + PLY CLADDING
3" OVERALL DEPTH

RAKED:
TEXTURED
TOP (IS WALKED
ON BY MOLLY-
NEEDS TO
SUPPORT
WEIGHT)

* SUNDIAL *

TEXTURE

GARDEN AREA
BARK/MULCH
SET INTO
PLASTER/CEMENT

OVERHEAD LINE OF
PROS. MOULDING
SUPPORTS WINDOW
(SKELETAL FRAME)

MAIN FLOOR AREA
RAKED

FLOOR TIMBER
PLANKS IN GROUPS
OF 4 × 6" WIDE

TEXTURE

BLACK
CARPET
AREA

EXIT/
ENTRANCE

BLACK
CARPET
AREA

EXIT/
ENTRANCE

CURTAIN

SCENE DESIGN
"MOLLY SWEENEY"

(DESIGNED BY JOE VANEK FOR ROUNDABOUT THEATRE COMPANY)

NEW PLAYS

★ HONOUR by Joanna Murray-Smith. In a series of intense confrontations, a wife, husband, lover and daughter negotiate the forces of passion, history, responsibility and honour. "HONOUR makes for surprisingly interesting viewing. Tight, crackling dialogue (usually played out in punchy verbal duels) captures characters unable to deal with emotions ... Murray-Smith effectively places her characters in situations that strip away pretense." –*Variety* "... the play's virtues are strong: a distinctive theatrical voice, passionate concerns ... HONOUR might just capture a few honors of its own." –*Time Out Magazine* [1M, 3W] ISBN: 0-8222-1683-3

★ MR. PETERS' CONNECTIONS by Arthur Miller. Mr. Miller describes the protagonist as existing in a dream-like state when the mind is "freed to roam from real memories to conjectures, from trivialities to tragic insights, from terror of death to glorying in one's being alive." With this memory play, the Tony Award and Pulitzer Prize-winner reaffirms his stature as the world's foremost dramatist. "... a cross between Joycean stream-of-consciousness and Strindberg's dream plays, sweetened with a dose of William Saroyan's philosophical whimsy ... CONNECTIONS is most intriguing ..." –*The NY Times* [5M, 3W] ISBN: 0-8222-1687-6

★ THE WAITING ROOM by Lisa Loomer. Three women from different centuries meet in a doctor's waiting room in this dark comedy about the timeless quest for beauty – and its cost. "... THE WAITING ROOM ... is a bold, risky melange of conflicting elements that is ... terrifically moving ... There's no resisting the fierce emotional pull of the play." –*The NY Times* "... one of the high points of this year's Off-Broadway season ... THE WAITING ROOM is well worth a visit." –*Back Stage* [7M, 4W, flexible casting] ISBN: 0-8222-1594-2

★ THE OLD SETTLER by John Henry Redwood. A sweet-natured comedy about two church-going sisters in 1943 Harlem and the handsome young man who rents a room in their apartment. "For all of its decent sentiments, THE OLD SETTLER avoids sentimentality. It has the authenticity and lack of pretense of an Early American sampler." –*The NY Times* "We've had some fine plays Off-Broadway this season, and this is one of the best." –*The NY Post* [1M, 3W] ISBN: 0-8-222-1642-6

★ THE LAST TRAIN TO NIBROC by Arlene Hutton. In 1940 two young strangers share a seat on a train bound east only to find their paths will cross again. "All aboard. LAST TRAIN TO NIBROC is a sweetly told little chamber romance." –*Show Business* "... [a] gently charming little play, reminiscent of Thorton Wilder in its look at rustic Americans who are to be treasured for their simplicity and directness ..." –*Associated Press* "The old formula of boy wins girls, boy loses girl, boy wins girl still works ... [a] well-made play that perfectly captures a slice of small-town-life-gone-by." –*Back Stage* [1M, 1W] ISBN: 0-8222-1753-8

★ OVER THE RIVER AND THROUGH THE WOODS by Joe DiPietro. Nick sees both sets of his grandparents every Sunday for dinner. This is routine until he has to tell them that he's been offered a dream job in Seattle. The news doesn't sit so well. "A hilarious family comedy that is even funnier than his long running musical revue *I Love You, You're Perfect, Now Change.*" –*Back Stage* "Loaded with laughs every step of the way." –*Star-Ledger* [3M, 3W] ISBN: 0-8222-1712-0

★ SIDE MAN by Warren Leight. 1999 Tony Award winner. This is the story of a broken family and the decline of jazz as popular entertainment. "... a tender, deeply personal memory play about the turmoil in the family of a jazz musician as his career crumbles at the dawn of the age of rock-and-roll ..." –*The NY Times* "[SIDE MAN] is an elegy for two things – a lost world and a lost love. When the two notes sound together in harmony, it is moving and graceful ..." –*The NY Daily News* "An atmospheric memory play...with crisp dialogue and clearly drawn characters ... reflects the passing of an era with persuasive insight ... The joy and despair of the musicians is skillfully illustrated." –*Variety* [5M, 3W] ISBN: 0-8222-1721-X

DRAMATISTS PLAY SERVICE, INC.
440 Park Avenue South, New York, NY 10016 212-683-8960 Fax 212-213-1539
postmaster@dramatists.com www.dramatists.com

NEW PLAYS

★ **CLOSER by Patrick Marber.** Winner of the 1998 Olivier Award for Best Play and the 1999 New York Drama Critics Circle Award for Best Foreign Play. Four lives intertwine over the course of four and a half years in this densely plotted, stinging look at modern love and betrayal. "CLOSER is a sad, savvy, often funny play that casts a steely, unblinking gaze at the world of relationships and lets you come to your own conclusions ... CLOSER does not merely hold your attention; it burrows into you." *–New York Magazine* "A powerful, darkly funny play about the cosmic collision between the sun of love and the comet of desire." *–Newsweek Magazine* [2M, 2W] ISBN: 0-8222-1722-8

★ **THE MOST FABULOUS STORY EVER TOLD by Paul Rudnick.** A stage manager, headset and prompt book at hand, brings the house lights to half, then dark, and cues the creation of the world. Throughout the play, she's in control of everything. In other words, she's either God, or she thinks she is. "Line by line, Mr. Rudnick may be the funniest writer for the stage in the United States today ... One-liners, epigrams, withering put-downs and flashing repartee: These are the candles that Mr. Rudnick lights instead of cursing the darkness ... a testament to the virtues of laughing ... and in laughter, there is something like the memory of Eden." *–The NY Times* "Funny it is ... consistently, rapaciously, deliriously ... easily the funniest play in town." *–Variety* [4M, 5W] ISBN: 0-8222-1720-1

★ **A DOLL'S HOUSE by Henrik Ibsen, adapted by Frank McGuinness.** Winner of the 1997 Tony Award for Best Revival. "New, raw, gut-twisting and gripping. Easily the hottest drama this season." *–USA Today* "Bold, brilliant and alive." *–The Wall Street Journal* "A thunderclap of an evening that takes your breath away." *–Time Magazine* [4M, 4W, 2 boys] ISBN: 0-8222-1636-1

★ **THE HERBAL BED by Peter Whelan.** The play is based on actual events which occurred in Stratford-upon-Avon in the summer of 1613, when William Shakespeare's elder daughter was publicly accused of having a sexual liaison with a married neighbor and family friend. "In his probing new play, THE HERBAL BED ... Peter Whelan muses about a sidelong event in the life of Shakespeare's family and creates a finely textured tapestry of love and lies in the early 17th-century Stratford." *–The NY Times* "It is a first rate drama with interesting moral issues of truth and expediency." *–The NY Post* [5M, 3W] ISBN: 0-8222-1675-2

★ **SNAKEBIT by David Marshall Grant.** A study of modern friendship when put to the test. "... a rather smart and absorbing evening of water-cooler theater, the intimate sort of Off-Broadway experience that has you picking apart the recognizable characters long after the curtain calls." *– The NY Times* "Off-Broadway keeps on presenting us with compelling reasons for going to the theater. The latest is SNAKEBIT, David Marshall Grant's smart new comic drama about being thirtysomething and losing one's way in life." *–The NY Daily News* [3M, 1W] ISBN: 0-8222-1724-4

★ **A QUESTION OF MERCY by David Rabe.** The Obie Award-winning playwright probes the sensitive and controversial issue of doctor-assisted suicide in the age of AIDS in this poignant drama. "There are many devastating ironies in Mr. Rabe's beautifully considered, piercingly clear-eyed work ..." *–The NY Times* "With unsettling candor and disturbing insight, the play arouses pity and understanding of a troubling subject ... Rabe's provocative tale is an affirmation of dignity that rings clear and true." *–Variety* [6M, 1W] ISBN: 0-8222-1643-4

★ **DIMLY PERCEIVED THREATS TO THE SYSTEM by Jon Klein.** Reality and fantasy overlap with hilarious results as this unforgettable family attempts to survive the nineties. "Here's a play whose point about fractured families goes to the heart, mind – and ears." *–The Washington Post* "... an end-of-the millennium comedy about a family on the verge of a nervous breakdown ... Trenchant and hilarious ..." *–The Baltimore Sun* [2M, 4W] ISBN: 0-8222-1677-9

DRAMATISTS PLAY SERVICE, INC.
440 Park Avenue South, New York, NY 10016 212-683-8960 Fax 212-213-1539
postmaster@dramatists.com www.dramatists.com

NEW PLAYS

★ **AS BEES IN HONEY DROWN by Douglas Carter Beane.** Winner of the John Gassner Playwriting Award. A hot young novelist finds the subject of his new screenplay in a New York socialite who leads him into the world of *Auntie Mame* and *Breakfast at Tiffany's*, before she takes him for a ride. "A delicious soufflé of a satire … [an] extremely entertaining fable for an age that always chooses image over substance." *–The NY Times* "… A witty assessment of one of the most active and relentless industries in a consumer society … the creation of 'hot' young things, which the media have learned to mass produce with efficiency and zeal." *–The NY Daily News* [3M, 3W, flexible casting] ISBN: 0-8222-1651-5

★ **STUPID KIDS by John C. Russell.** In rapid, highly stylized scenes, the story follows four high-school students as they make their way from first through eighth period and beyond, struggling with the fears, frustrations, and longings peculiar to youth. "In STUPID KIDS … playwright John C. Russell gets the opera of adolescence to a T … The stylized teenspeak of STUPID KIDS … suggests that Mr. Russell may have hidden a tape recorder under a desk in study hall somewhere and then scoured the tapes for good quotations … it is the kids' insular, ceaselessly churning world, a pre-adult world of Doritos and libidos, that the playwright seeks to lay bare." *–The NY Times* "STUPID KIDS [is] a sharp-edged … whoosh of teen angst and conformity anguish. It is also very funny." *–NY Newsday* [2M, 2W] ISBN: 0-8222-1698-1

★ **COLLECTED STORIES by Donald Margulies.** From Obie Award-winner Donald Margulies comes a provocative analysis of a student-teacher relationship that turns sour when the protégé becomes a rival. "With his fine ear for detail, Margulies creates an authentic, insular world, and he gives equal weight to the opposing viewpoints of two formidable characters." *–The LA Times* "This is probably Margulies' best play to date …" *–The NY Post* "… always fluid and lively, the play is thick with ideas, like a stock-pot of good stew." *–The Village Voice* [2W] ISBN: 0-8222-1640-X

★ **FREEDOMLAND by Amy Freed.** An overdue showdown between a son and his father sets off fireworks that illuminate the neurosis, rage and anxiety of one family – and of America at the turn of the millennium. "FREEDOMLAND's more obvious links are to *Buried Child* and *Bosoms and Neglect*. Freed, like Guare, is an inspired wordsmith with a gift for surreal touches in situations grounded in familiar and real territory." *–Curtain Up* [3M, 4W] ISBN: 0-8222-1719-8

★ **STOP KISS by Diana Son.** A poignant and funny play about the ways, both sudden and slow, that lives can change irrevocably. "There's so much that is vital and exciting about STOP KISS … you want to embrace this young author and cheer her onto other works … the writing on display here is funny and credible … you also will be charmed by its heartfelt characters and up-to-the-minute humor." *–The NY Daily News* "… irresistibly exciting … a sweet, sad, and enchantingly sincere play." *–The NY Times* [3M, 3W] ISBN: 0-8222-1731-7

★ **THREE DAYS OF RAIN by Richard Greenberg.** The sins of fathers and mothers make for a bittersweet elegy in this poignant and revealing drama. "… a work so perfectly judged it heralds the arrival of a major playwright … Greenberg is extraordinary." *–The NY Daily News* "Greenberg's play is filled with graceful passages that are by turns melancholy, harrowing, and often, quite funny." *–Variety* [2M, 1W] ISBN: 0-8222-1676-0

★ **THE WEIR by Conor McPherson.** In a bar in rural Ireland, the local men swap spooky stories in an attempt to impress a young woman from Dublin who recently moved into a nearby "haunted" house. However, the tables are soon turned when she spins a yarn of her own. "You shed all sense of time at this beautiful and devious new play." *–The NY Times* "Sheer theatrical magic. I have rarely been so convinced that I have just seen a modern classic. Tremendous." *–The London Daily Telegraph* [4M, 1W] ISBN: 0-8222-1706-6

DRAMATISTS PLAY SERVICE, INC.
440 Park Avenue South, New York, NY 10016 212-683-8960 Fax 212-213-1539
postmaster@dramatists.com www.dramatists.com